BLINDSIDED

Dawn Downey
11/14/20

BLINDSIDED

Essays from the Only
Black Woman in the Room

DAWN DOWNEY

Published 2020 by Pathless Land Press
Printed in the United States of America

ISBN 978-0-9963240-7-6

Cover design by Book Cover Express
www.BookCoverExpress.com

Book design by Maureen Cutajar
www.gopublished.com

Author photo by Jacob Meyer
New Friends Photography
vimeo.com/jacobjmeyer

Some names were changed for privacy and because the author can barely remember her own name.

For Ben, my sunshine

ACKNOWLEDGMENTS

Thank you for reading *Blindsided*.

Previous versions of "Good People" and "The N Word" appeared in *Stumbling Toward the Buddha: Stories about Tripping over My Principles on the Road to Transformation*.

"Comfort Food" was first published by *River, Blood, and Corn Literary Journal*

"Seduced" appeared in *Searching for My Heart: Essays about Love*.

"The Cleaning Women" was first published by *punctuate*.

Thank you to the following people who supported me while I wrote this book:

Developmental/Content Editor, Jessica Conoley

Copy Editor, Julie Tenenbaum, owner of Final Draft Secretarial Service

Critique group, Jessica Conoley and Jim Cosgrove

Everyone who opens the Friday email from Dawn Downey's Writing. There is no bigger contribution to an author's creativity than expecting her to sit down and get to work.

Cheryl Wilfong has spread my writing far and wide via her blog, The Meditative Gardener. Countless readers have found my essays through Cheryl's generosity.

Dan Blank of We Grow Media. Through his weekly newsletter, he encourages me toward radical clarity about why I write and who it's for. Clarity of purpose made this a better book.

Kelli Austin, Carolyn Celestine, Jessica Conoley, Victor J. Dougherty, Katherine Guendling, Lisa Sinicki, Margaret Towner, and Ben Worth chose the cover design. Out of six design options, their choice was unanimous. Thank goodness my vote didn't count.

Angelique Downey Robinson created Jazzy and transformed how I see myself in the world.

TABLE OF CONTENTS

PROLOGUE

Soul Music

The first week of ninth grade at my new high school, I scurried down the hallway, tail between my legs. Black girls loitered in a pack, arms crossed, hips jutted. One of them popped her gum at me. "High yellow bitch."

My knees buckled.

I didn't know what *high yellow* meant, but I understood *bitch*.

Please let the bell ring.

I should have detoured to my locker before third period social studies.

Please let the bell ring.

I should have skipped first period swimming, so at least I wouldn't have to hide my nappy roots under a headscarf.

Please let the bell ring.

I should have been born with hair that knew how to act, that dipped and swirled like the bouffant on the girl who'd popped her gum at me.

That summer, my family had moved from Des Moines to Pasadena.

I went from buckeye trees, which dropped rock-hard seeds for the bully down the street to throw at me, to palm trees that spiked from the concrete and soared into the sky like pitchforks stabbing the sun. From Mama to a white stepmother. From junior high where I'd been nameless, to high school where my name was High Yellow Bitch.

Teachers at John Muir High School labeled me a high-potential/low-achiever and recommended my parents enroll me in Upward Bound.

Upward Bound—fancy words for summer school.

They were going to ship me off to Occidental College in Los Angeles for six weeks. Although summer away from home meant a reprieve from Dad yelling about my grades and stepmother Kim yelling about me hiding in my room in a cloud of incense smoke, I neither agreed with the idea nor fought it. It was a change, but not a choice.

～୨୧～

From Monday to Friday, we attended classes I hadn't paid attention to in school and classes that taught me how to study.

On weekends, we took field trips to places I'd never heard of.

We stepped off a school bus at the Hollywood Bowl and trooped through the parking lot to a reserved section at the back. Acres of white folding chairs were lined up in curved rows—a thousand moons, orbiting a lawn so evenly green it looked painted. Surrounding the green and white, a border of mounded flowers in reds and purples. It was as if I'd wandered into the Gauguin paintings my stepmother tried to get me to like.

I hooked my feet over the crossbar of the wooden chair. The program said *Swan Lake*. Margot Fonteyn. Rudolph Nureyev. Names that meant nothing. I turned the slick pages to photos of the corps de ballet. On page eight, a dancer was caught in mid-flight, her arms in a graceful arc that framed her feathered headdress. Her toes were pointed, her arches curved into semi-circles. From the upturned tilt of her chin, you could tell she would land exactly where she intended. As the sounds of the orchestra rolled across the grass, chatter subsided. The stage was tiny as a snow globe and the dancers a flurry of white. I leaned forward in my chair, all the way to intermission.

On the ride from Hollywood back to campus, I opened the program to the dancer caught in mid-flight. I smoothed the pages flat open in my lap, tilted my chin up, but not so much my seatmate would notice. I straightened one leg, and to the tune of grinding gears, pointed and flexed.

Bus rides squeezed us high-potential/low achievers together, which led to halting conversations. Another bus ride, another timid exchange. Week one, I learned faces. Week two, names. Week three, the stories behind the names and faces. Learn a name. Hear the story. Forget the name. Forget the story. Relearn the name. Relearn the story. Although our ages varied from sophomores to seniors, we were equally out of place. If you'd been in a clique at home, that was left behind. If you'd been ostracized from cliques at home, that was left behind, too. The Upward Bounders seemed inclined to give each other a chance. If they knew I was High Yellow Bitch, they didn't let on.

I was swept along when they sneaked out behind the dorm to smoke, and they watched me cough through my first cigarette. They taught me the power of smoky eyeliner. I learned if a boy grinned at me, to look at him sideways, frown, and strut away.

Jessie from Jefferson High shook her head at my hot-combed hair that frizzed up in the evening fog. She shampooed me in the bathroom sink, rubbing so hard my scalp moved around.

She asked, "You tender-headed?"

"Nu-uh."

~✺~

One Easter, when I was ten, Mama'd taken me to a beauty shop in an old lady's basement. The woman had yanked my head hard, not a single *you tender-headed, baby?* Working the hot comb through my hair, she'd burnt my ear, even though I was holding it folded over. No *sorry, baby*. Just as well, because I wouldn't have known what to do with a *sorry, baby*. Mama'd never asked about my possibly tender head; she'd never touched my hair.

~⌒~

I didn't know about tender, until Jessie from Jefferson High snugged a towel around my neck, until she wrapped the terry cloth into a turban, until she dabbed Prell-scented water from my forehead.

I sat on the floor between her legs, she on the bed, her knees pressed against my shoulders, holding me close. She greased my scalp like it was a cookie sheet and then stuffed my hair into the bonnet of a portable dryer to bake in the sweetness.

I emerged with a natural.

The natural felt like a poodle, but as light as the air that brushed my neck. I was free. Goodbye to running from rain, fog, and swimming pools. No more hiding nappy roots under a scarf. Jessie showed me how to use an Afro pick and how to pat wayward coils into place. Knowing what to do—that was freedom, too. She held up a mirror. The natural looked confident, a kinky basketball and just about as big. The natural refused to hide. Whose hair was that? I patted the top. My hair. My confidence.

On the afternoon of our first chaperoned party, we gathered in the dorm lounge to trade clothes. My dorm-mates tossed mini-skirts and blouses across the couches. A red dress dropped into my lap; Jessie was examining a pair of earrings, pretending it wasn't her who'd dropped it. I tried the dress on over my shorts. Twirling, I was the ballerina on page eight. For a minute, anyway. Too many eyes. I curled back down into an armchair.

Conversation filled the room like soul music.

"Sister, work that thing."

"Mmm. Hmm. He is fi-i-i-ne."

"That. Is boss. On you."

As soon as the radio blasted *nowhere to run to, nowhere to hide,* everybody jumped up. I stayed glued to the chair, until someone pulled me to my feet. I mimicked their hips, studied their snaky arms, and finally sneaked a glance at Jessie. She winked. Motown took me over, and I stepped steps I'd never stepped before, surrounded by half-dressed girls who danced like they wanted you to watch.

At the party, Stevie Wonder sang *I was made to love her.* A skinny boy took my hand. When the music told me how to sway and shimmy, the borrowed dress swished around my legs.

In my new bedroom, I dug through a box for incense and sank onto the floor, shoulders pressed against the closed door. Dresser and vanity were smashed up against each other, cowering in a corner. Weeks after we'd lugged all our belongings from a U-Haul, I still couldn't figure out how to arrange my furniture. At the close of Upward Bound, the friends who'd taught me to dance and smoke swore we'd meet up at football games, since our schools were cross-town rivals. But my family moved again, from Pasadena to Santa Barbara, two hours away. Arms wrapped around my knees, I hid in a cloud of sandalwood until school started.

On the way to Spanish class, I hugged the wall, but a gang of boys traipsing down the stairs stopped on cue. "Hey, fox." "Give a brother a chance."

I bit my lip.

"Don't be stuck up."

Too many. Too loud. Too close.

Pressed-hair sisters hovered nearby. A slicked-back ponytail sucked her teeth and cut her eyes at me. "Got 'em with that head, didn't you?"

That head? My natural? The sweetness Jessie'd baked into my hair turned bitter. Slick-Back Ponytail would never invite me to trade clothes. I didn't even speak her language. In my mouth *got 'em with that head* would come out *your hairdo attracted their attention.* I didn't know how to be one of the sisters—how to pop that gum and snap those fingers like *you better get outta my way.* As I stiffened, trying to make it to the end of the hall and the end of the day, my shoulder bag bumped against my hip.

Step, thump.

Please let the bell ring.

Step, thump.

Please let the bell ring.

Step, thump.

Please let the bell ring.

~⋅~

I sat cross-legged in the front yard, entertaining the family puppy, a yippy fluff ball with a wet nose on one end and brush tail on the other.

A girl my age walked by. "Hi. Darling puppy."

"Hi." What did she want?

"I'm Belinda. I live two houses down. Can I pet her?"

The puppy had already decided the answer was yes. She was in Belinda's lap in a yip and three bounces.

Belinda said, "I've seen you at school." We were in the same grade.

The puppy stood up in her lap, licking her chin like an ice cream cone.

"There's a party Saturday. Feel like going?"

Just the way Jesse'd asked, *you tender-headed,* before she'd rescued my hair, before dorm-mates had coaxed me onto my feet.

I nodded. "Um …okay."

"Come by at eight. I'm driving. Just got my license."

After she untangled herself and headed down the sidewalk, she looked back. "See you Saturday."

—⁓—

Cars lined the street, the summer night punctuated by as much "Hola" and "Mira, chica" as "Hi, Belinda."

Patting my Afro, I followed her into the house. I couldn't tell who actually lived there. Everybody knew where the bathroom was, and which bedroom to stash your purse in, and whose faces peered out from the photos on the dresser. Kids were picking through 45s stacked on the stereo console but eddied around Belinda as we passed.

In the kitchen, the music softened enough for introductions.

Belinda said, "Sylvio, this is Dawn. She moved in down the street from me."

Sylvio was pouring wine, Seven-Up, and ice into a punch bowl. He handed me a glass. "House on the corner?"

I took a sip. "Uh huh."

He passed another glass to someone behind me. "Angie, Dawn moved into that house on Voluntario."

"Nice to meet you. Righteous natural."

Belinda pulled me back into the living room, where she was swallowed in the dim light. When the Jackson Five did their ABCs, everybody sang along and grabbed partners. These kids sang soul music and danced like *Soul Train,* but to my Des Moines-trained eyes, they looked white. None of them looked like me.

Sylvio took my hand. I hesitated, then set down my glass, and after three fast songs and a slow one, forgot where.

Monday morning, Belinda and I walked to school together. Since we had different schedules, she said, "Bye. Call you tonight," as soon as we set foot inside the packed hall.

The vice principal stood guard in his doorway, ready to send me home if my skirt didn't reach my knees. The pressed-hair sisters, wearing matching sneers, advanced straight for me, their maybe-boyfriends close behind, who leered and pointed in my direction. Dared each other in low rumbles that croaked in the middle to high-pitched. Lockers slammed. The warning bell clanged. Announcements blared. I squeezed through to the edge of the crowd and stumbled over to the wall, right into the path of a teacher rushing by. His armload of books exploded at my feet.

Somebody stumbled over me. "Get out of the way."

Please let the bell ring.

I looked up. "Sorry."

Please let the bell ring.

The somebody had already vanished, but the looking tricked me into a straighter posture.

Please let—

I rocked back onto my heels. I felt too light. Had I dropped my purse … books? No, still here in the crook of my arm. I rose to standing. Five-feet-one was taller than before. There was more space inside my skin. Something … familiar … missing. A sense of threat—I wasn't waiting to be attacked.

Maybe it would last only a minute or two, but I felt the absence as clearly as when a bully leaves the room.

Was this a trick? I needed to get my bearings.

The teacher raced off, his books corralled without my help. The vice principal stopped one of the pressed-hair sisters and was giving her a pink slip, as her girlfriends rushed past. The boys disappeared into classrooms, not a single glance in my direction. By the time announcements trailed off to "tryouts for *Sound of Music* after fifth period," only a few stragglers remained, among them Angie from Saturday's party. She waved. I mouthed *hi*. The clock above the office warned hurry up, hurry up, hurry up, but its warning went unheeded. I wanted to find my own rhythm.

When the tardy bell rang, it clanged through a hallway as empty as a dance floor before the first song.

I patted my Afro and marched off to homeroom.

PART ONE

THE N WORD:

A PRAYER OF THANKSGIVING

After Thanksgiving dinner, candles flickered hypnotic shadows across my living room walls. Dessert plates and wine glasses cluttered the coffee table. I perched on a hassock, in a relaxed version of "The Thinker," my legs uncrossed. I'd given up the comfortable seats to my companions—friends who were members of my meditation group. Our relationships forged from the inside out, I knew little about their personal histories, but we shared a curiosity about the Ultimate Mystery.

Around the coffee table, we'd unconsciously formed a circle, as we did every week. If a bell had sounded, we would have slipped right into the silence.

Grant, stiff and angular as Origami, had claimed the wooden rocker to my left. Opera was Grant's hobby, and when the acoustics of a room tempted him, he turned into an Italian tenor. It was always a treat for me to watch him fall in love with his favorite music, during every impromptu performance.

Slouched in an overstuffed chair directly across from me was Ben, prone to observing from the background at parties. We were a couple in a tenuous stage. Still finding our way together, as yet unsure about the direction of our commitment.

Grant's wife curled up in a chair next to Ben.

Opposite Grant, Rhonda snuggled into the couch. She caressed the velvet as she lamented her unsuccessful attempts to find a girl-friend. She and I occasionally met for lunch, where we explored secret corners of our lives—the hurts that had turned us into spiritual seekers.

Another married couple was squeezed in next to Rhonda on the sofa, completing our accidental circle.

For the evening, dharma discussions were set aside, while we gossiped about celebrities. The Internet had buzzed in outrage that week, over a white stand-up comic who had shouted racial slurs at black hecklers. We shook our heads and tut-tutted his behavior.

"… can't imagine what he was thinking."

"… showed his ignorance."

"… worse than the hecklers."

I wished one of my guests would ask, *so Dawn, as an African-American woman, what do you think?* But they were tripping over their color-blindness, going out of their way to act as though I were one of them. I felt like the elephant in the middle of the room, worried that somebody was about to make an elephant joke.

I crossed my ankles.

Grant folded his hands in his lap and bowed his head. When he raised his gaze, he seemed to focus inward, like the pause before an aria. "My dad was racist. He called his employees niggers."

I froze. Fifty-some years old, and I was right back in junior high. American history. The section on slavery. The feeling my classmates had shifted at their desks to get a better look at me, a real life descendant of slaves.

I stared at Grant. The slightest twitch, and everyone's attention would turn to me. His expression gave away no sign that he objected to the fact his dad was a racist … no sign that he worried about my reaction to the word … no sign that he cared about me. If only he would flinch.

He didn't. Grant said *nigger* like he'd said it 10,000 times before.

"Yeah, my dad, too." It was Rhonda, on the couch. She was hugging one of my chenille pillows. "Nigger, all the time."

I glanced in her direction, catching Ben in my peripheral vision. I wanted him to rescue me, but his posture was unchanged, as though he hadn't heard. Unwilling to acknowledge the doubts and questions now swirling between us, I blinked him out of view.

My tongue turned into a thick, dry lump. Hands went cold, face hot. I braced myself, certain the first two blows portended a third.

Speak up, Dawn. But speaking up meant risking a scene. My whole life, I'd been taught *Don't make a scene.*

If only the evening would rewind to fifteen minutes earlier, when I had been safe and my guests had been innocent. The *N* word had just downgraded them from *friends* to *them,* people from whom I needed protection.

In college, my classmates, who'd grown up in poor black neighborhoods, had insisted, "You can't trust white people. No way. No how." I had disagreed. If that were true, you'd have to indict half my family. My white stepmother, who I'd promoted to Mother on the day she and Dad drove me to college. Younger brother. Baby sister. Maternal great-grandmother. And the Downey who had probably owned my paternal great-great-grandfather. As I grew older, mistrust grew. I suspected all (most? some? how do you arrive at an estimation?) white people sprinkled racial slurs into their conversations, within the confines of their private lives. My suspicion congealed as I attended on-the-job diversity workshops and after-work cocktail parties. It seemed the more I got to know acquaintances who were white, the closer I got to a danger zone … where they forgot … perhaps … that a non-club-member was in the room. And then a comment slipped out.

What shattered me was the ease with which it slipped.

~ ❧ ~

On Thanksgiving, my mood muffled the small talk, like a radio station just out of range, until the evening lumbered to an end.

The scene haunted me. Grant's dour expression. Rhonda hugging my pillow.

The next few days, I waited. Ben should care enough to bring it up. No, I should bring it up. No, he should.

I waited for the others to call, to say, "I'm sorry Grant and Rhonda were so insensitive." Or "hope you're okay." Maybe they'd been afraid to voice their sympathy that night. Maybe they'd find the courage in a phone call or email. Maybe they'd been brought up like me: *Don't make a scene*. But the phone remained dead quiet, the in-box empty.

I waited for anger to fire up. Wouldn't it feel better to throw something? At whom? Grant and Rhonda, for saying it? Me, for not speaking up? Ben, for not rescuing me?

Buried under a comforter, I lay in bed slipping restlessly toward sleep, when hurt, betrayal, and rage erupted in a shudder. I flung back the comforter. Kicked at the sheets. Beat up the mattress. I cursed out the entire white world. After words could no longer express my feelings, I screamed into my pillow—the trumpeting of a wounded elephant.

My tangled bedding was damp from tears and sweat. It would never end. I would never be safe.

Hopeless.

You get to hopeless by sinking.

I sank through dreamlike images of shackles, chains, branding irons, whips, ropes, nightsticks, burning crosses, and fire hoses. Bloodhounds on my trail, police dogs at my throat. I crashed through all the places that are supposed to be safe: school yards, lunch counters, court-houses, and church basements. From nigger to nigra to colored to negro to black to african-american and back again. Strange fruit. Centuries-old images absorbed from textbooks. Civil rights marches flickering across the family television. Labels, passed down from one generation to the next, labels meant to hold me apart—the other.

The storm subsided. On the other side of hopeless, there was calm.

I got up, washed my face, and then climbed back into bed. Sleep overtook me but revealed an unwelcome path forward. I had to talk to them.

The Buddha said, "Take refuge in the sangha." Your community. It was a double paradox. First, *the sangha* had ambushed me on Thanksgiving. Second, I doubted the great teacher intended refuge as a place of safety. He would have shaken his head at the notion of protecting myself. Protecting who?

The Buddha did not advise me to turn away from conflict. His teachings assured that if I examined my experiences, good and bad, I'd discover something pure. He challenged me to look for myself, rather than accept his words untested. I was compelled to look, compelled to unravel the Mystery.

Rhonda and I went out to dinner, a date we'd scheduled weeks before Thanksgiving. After our meal, she would accompany me to a magazine launch, where she'd be my cheerleader while I read. I pushed broccoli around the plate, pleased Rhonda wanted to support my performance, but also worried about broaching the subject of the *N*

word. She might protest or label me hypersensitive. I could end up feeling worse.

"Not sure how to say this. Thanksgiving night ... I felt attacked ... you said — "

The flash of recognition on her face stopped me.

She clenched her gut. "Oh God. I feel like that when somebody says *dyke*."

We both winced. The word encompassed all the slurs I'd overheard about lesbians, as well as those I'd endured about myself.

She touched my hand. "I'm so sorry."

Neither of us moved, even our breath too quiet to trouble the peaceful space that held us.

She nodded. "Thank you," she said.

I didn't understand the thank you, but my intuition said the understanding was irrelevant.

~ ❀ ~

I approached Grant after a Sunday morning meditation. "Remember Thanksgiving? What you said ... it hurt me ... still hurts."

He towered over me by a foot. "I certainly didn't mean to. I'm sorry if I did." His expression betrayed no emotion.

I walked away, disappointed, but resigned. I'd done my best. In fact, the apology was his best, too. Time to let it go.

Wednesday evening after another group sit, I'd buttoned up my coat and was waving "see you next week" to the regulars, when Grant tapped me on the shoulder. His eyes brimmed. His voice cracked. "You really got to me. That night I was talking about my dad. But I see myself. It's painful. Realizing how hard my heart is. I'm deeply sorry ... and I want to thank you."

His face was flushed, but his gaze was soft. Surrounded by empty chairs and the bustle of departing friends, we recognized each other.

And Ben. I was afraid to talk to him, because it was bigger than race. It was about relationship. The conversations with Rhonda and Grant had tempered my desperation for rescue and given rise to an unfamiliar sensation: I wanted to understand Ben, as much as I wanted him to understand me. I'd never felt that way about a man. I appreciated this new awareness. The road ahead loomed with difficulties for us, but for the first time, I saw the road.

It would never end. I'd never be safe. And yet, the gratitude Rhonda and Grant had expressed had enveloped me as well. I was mystified. In the collision of our lives, I discovered something pure: an alchemy that transformed profanities into prayers of thanksgiving.

Comfort Food

The to-go box on the kitchen counter held a piece of apple pie, a reward for toiling at my computer all morning after a breakfast date with my husband. I savored the anticipation as much as I was about to savor the pie. I imagined the treat nestled inside the box—a deep wedge of sweetness, the peaks of the crust a golden brown and the valleys glinting with sugar. It would be overstuffed with thick filling, an apple slice or two escaping the triangle. How the house would fill with the sweet aroma of hot apple pie when I warmed it in the oven. Fork in hand, I opened the box. Staring me in the face was a pile of burnt crust pieces and goop that looked like something swept up from the floor. You call this pie?

Assholes. I can't believe they pulled this. I should have checked the box before we left. No. I shouldn't have to check. Maybe they didn't pull anything. Sometimes pie comes out of the pan messy. Don't make excuses for them. You might give this to a relative, not to a customer. Who did it? And did they know who the customer was? Assholes.

As my husband and I pulled into the parking lot of a neighborhood cafe, freezing wind whipped the Stars and Stripes around a flagpole.

The lot was packed with pick-ups, except for four off-duty police cruisers. I shoved my hands into my pockets and used Ben as a wind-break, crossing the lot. The restaurant, a red barn with green awnings, was the kind of place frequented by regulars, which did not include me—my experience limited to one catfish lunch. Ben had eaten there with a buddy often enough to know the menu included his favorites.

A bakery case spotlighted cobbler, cake, cinnamon rolls, and golden wedges of apple pie. The cops lounged at a round table, heads bowed, fingers at work on the keys of their cell phones. I scanned the room for non-white faces (there were none) and simultaneously chastised myself for the automatic reaction. Beside the pass-through to the kitchen, a life-sized wooden pig held a sign ordering *Eat More Chicken*. Above the case, another sign boasted *Home Cookin'*. Just what I needed. Comfort food. In comfort food cafés, the servers were efficient, and they always called me honey. I had a soft spot for both qualities.

A hostess approached, her expression set in a snarl. She glanced in my direction just long enough to ignore me, then shifted her slitty-eyed attention to a spot near Ben's feet. "Two?" she asked.

I knew that move. My sister and I had used it on each other whenever we were feuding.

The hostess might have intended the attitude for me in particular, or she might have intended it for both of us. It was also possible that a general bad mood had plastered the sneer on her face before we walked in. Ben didn't seem to notice, much female nonverbal communication being under the male radar. He pointed to a vintage motorcycle balanced on top of a waist-high room divider. "Yeah, two. There's a spot I like over by the Indian."

She'd already shuffled off toward stools lined up at a counter. She veered from her original course and headed toward the divider.

Ben said, "I mean the other side. It's quieter. That okay?"

"Wherever you want." She had her back to us, but I could tell she was rolling her eyes. She led us to a booth, where she dropped two menus onto the table. "Your waitress …" Her departure muffled the remainder of the sentence.

A hook poked from a nearby coat rack, so I reached out to hang my parka. A customer was sitting across the room, glaring over her shoulder at me. I was used to catching an initial gawk when I walked into a room, and then the gawker's face usually warmed into an embarrassed smile. This woman was ice. She spooked me. She parted her lips, and her companion slow-motioned his stare in my direction. I refused to turn away. Mouths set in twin grimaces, they stared for as long as it took me to hang my coat and fumble out of scarf and hat. I'd seen the expression before—on a couple of good ole boys in a little mountain town. They'd been sitting on chairs outside a pool hall, their legs stretched across the sidewalk, blocking my progress. They waited a beat, then slow-motioned their resentful legs out of the way.

When I shuddered into the booth, the placement of the table put my back to the couple. Damned if I didn't land in the path of another poison arrow. The woman sat by herself in a corner, elbows on her table, coffee cup cradled in her hands. Eyes narrowed, she peered through the steam rising from her cup. Her shoulders were squared as she leaned forward, facing me head-on. She didn't break eye contact. I was shocked. It was the glare that a guy in a rusted pick-up had used on me years before—both of us stopped at a red light. He'd made eye contact, held it, and then spat out his window.

Ben studied his menu.

I simmered.

If I mentioned the incidents, how would the conversation go? Me: These people are staring at me. Ben: Of course. You're beautiful. Me: It's not funny. And then I'd pitch a fit. Or, Me: That couple looks like they want to kill me. Ben: Honey, I'm sorry. Want to go somewhere else? Me: What? Let them chase me off? And then I'd pitch a fit. Or, Me: That woman's giving me a dirty look. Ben: What do you need from me? Me: Nothing, something, I don't know. And then I'd pitch a fit. And then the table full of cops would be all over me. I couldn't unravel my tangled emotions on the spot. Better to bury the knot under pancakes.

Our server walked over. She was blue-collar skinny, and my tension parted in the wake of her unhurried ease. Penny, according to her name tag. "How are you folks, this morning?" She filled Ben's cup without needing to ask him, warmth radiating from more than the coffee pot. "Need another minute?"

I pointed to Number 6 on the menu. "Nope. Pancakes and eggs."

"How you want your egg, honey?"

Servers who called me honey always took good care of me.

I relaxed. "Scrambled."

Ben said, "Biscuits and gravy."

Before I had time to enumerate the ways that choice would shorten his lifespan, Penny had already set our plates in front of us. "I'll be back to check on you."

After the pancakes did their job, I sipped hot tea. A border of chickens marched along the top of the restaurant walls, complemented by vintage tin signs. *We Feed Our Chickens Gooch's Best,* bragged one. I chuckled at another, a hen that proclaimed *He Rules the Roost, But I Rule the Rooster.* My rooster and I solved the world's problems, in between groans of satisfaction. Penny breezed by again to top off Ben's cup. It seemed her timing was set by a secret code that passed between coffee-drinkers and servers. I shook my head in wonder at the magic of the transaction, as she walked into the second dining room. "How does she—?"

Above the doorway, next to *Sweet Lassy Feeds,* hung a movie poster for *Gone With the Wind.*

But I did not see Scarlet O'Hara and Rhett Butler. I saw bloody stripes on naked ebony backs.

I did not see a love story, I saw slavery.

Despair and anger threatened to boil over. Here I was, on a spontaneous date with my sweetie; it had been my idea. Hell, I'd even picked the place. If I succumbed to my feelings, then the restaurant won. If I shared my feelings with Ben, the restaurant won anyway, by controlling my conversation. I would tell Ben later, at home. The restaurant would not win.

A phantom self, covered in the slime of partially-digested insults, slipped from her tomb deep within my belly. While I caressed my hubby's fingertips, the phantom wailed, smashed plates, and threw chairs. She ripped the poster from the wall and set fire to—

Penny was gathering up our dirty dishes. "Honey, you got room for dessert?"

"Apple pie, please. To go."

Fork in hand, I opened the to-go box on my kitchen counter. Inside was a heap of burnt crust pieces and goop.

They'd thrown scraps into my pastry carton.

Scraps where there ought to be pie. But sometimes pie comes out of the pan messy. Don't make excuses. But who filled the box? Maybe they didn't know who the customer was. Maybe this is just about sloppy customer service. Yeah. Maybe.

I was sick of the constant onslaught. Little things. Big things. Cops repeatedly pulling me over two blocks from my house for two miles over the speed limit. People who bragged they were color-blind. Magazine covers—their dark-skinned celebrities photo-shopped four shades lighter. Pairing up in diversity training class, my white colleagues picked each other and left me standing alone, the diversity trainer and me staring our disbelief/belief at each other. The neighbor who'd confronted me on my daily walk. "I've never seen you.

Where do you live?" The straight-haired acquaintance who coveted my nappy-hair dreadlocks, but she sure didn't covet my nappy-hair life. I was a news story on a loop: assault, protest, investigation, no indictment, protest, silence. Repeat.

Maybe they hadn't known who'd ordered dessert to-go. Yeah. Maybe. I lay my fork beside the open box.

White privilege: the ability to attribute mangled pie to bad service.

GOOD PEOPLE

Harmony Vineyard Church. Summer. Ben and I visited on a whim the first time; we lived just down the road. We returned because he liked the music and I liked tagging along on my husband's whims, but I was wary. White churches made me nervous.

The preacher read the announcements from the bulletin and chuckled about the typos he encountered. "This must have been written by some illiterate Italian who can't speak English."

I elbowed Ben. "Did you hear that? He just made a racist joke."

"I know … yeah …"

Ben was alarmed, but not as mad as I was.

When the minister said "illiterate Italian," I heard *nigger*.

Hogan Preparatory Academy. Autumn. Crossing the midtown high school campus in search of the football stadium, I was self-conscious. I'd probably be the only African American at the game rooting for the white school. My nephew was their star wide receiver.

I would join my neighbors and chat about life in the suburbs, split-level homes built on lawns too big for us to maintain sans lawn service. I'd ask if mums were on sale yet at the nursery they'd recommended when I first moved in, which would lead to grousing that the perennial bed at the house around the corner put mine to shame. We would grow solemn about the team's slim chance for victory over Hogan Prep, our boys going up against the state champs, who had a home field advantage to boot.

~ ◯ ~

Harmony Vineyard Church. The unyielding pew pressed against my back.

I composed a rebuttal sermon to the minister, peppered with *how-dare-yous* and *shame-on-yous* and a fusillade of *you-don't-knows*. But maybe I should give him the benefit of the doubt. Let the whole thing drop. We'd never come back here, anyway. I fidgeted. Parishioners flipped through hymnals; some yawned, like it was an ordinary Sunday. I drummed my fingers on Ben's knee. Why didn't they stand up and demand an apology? Probably because they agreed with the slur. Because the insult *was* ordinary. Because they didn't want me here. If they hated Italians, they sure as hell hated me. It was no longer Kansas City, 2003. It was Montgomery, 1961.

~ ◯ ~

Hogan Prep Academy. Three black teenagers sauntered toward me, dressed in baggy pants and shirts that hung to their knees. Shoulder punching emphasized their banter, laced with an occasional "Dude" and "Bro."

When they were close, I asked, "Scuze me, is the football field this way?"

"Yes, ma'am. If you continue down the walkway, you'll find it directly on your left," one of them said.

And then all three in unison. "Have a nice day."

"Thanks, you too." My brows furrowed, I headed in the direction they pointed. Something seemed odd, like a video playback had glitched. I paused and looked over my shoulder.

They were still poking, still teasing, their voices fading into the autumn breeze.

The video rewound. I smacked my forehead. "Oh, no."

<hr>

Harmony Vineyard Church. After the service, I said, "I'm going down to meet the minister."

Ben chuckled. "Right. I'll bet you are."

It tickled him when I got feisty and stood up for myself. The idea of little me taking down this preacher puffed up my husband with pride. His pride was misplaced. Although my squared shoulders signaled confidence, I was trembling.

I trudged down the aisle to the front of the sanctuary, where the pastor stood greeting his flock. He smiled when we shook hands.

I pushed my dreadlocks off my face. "We ... my husband and I ... visited last Sunday ... and today. We felt welcome ... until that joke about Italians. I don't feel welcome anymore."

His smile dissolved.

"Oh. Let me explain. We're doing a pizza fundraiser with an Italian restaurant and—"

"I'm not here to accuse you of anything. Or make assumptions about your motives." Maybe there was still a way to let him off the hook, to end this awkward exchange. I usually shrank away from conflict. I shocked myself—standing firm. "That remark ... it made me think ... when will it be my turn? When will you all make fun of me?"

"That won't ever happen. When you get to know me better, you'll understand."

One arm open, gesturing to an unseen audience, he recited his accomplishments in the area of diversity. He listed the church's contributions to civic committees, initiatives on behalf of immigrants, and programs for inner city youth. It sounded like a presentation to the Chamber of Commerce.

"I'm new to your church. Didn't know you when you made the joke."

He dropped his arm to his side. He shifted his weight from one foot to the other. He cleared his throat.

My temples throbbed.

He sighed. "I apologize. It wasn't very smart. Thank you for your courage … and honesty." He draped his arm across my shoulders, uninvited. "I hope you and your husband will come back."

I cringed and took a step backward.

Hogan Prep Academy. A gust of wind blew leaves across the walkway.

I was stunned by those boys, because they sounded like college professors instead of gangster rappers.

I cringed at my assumptions and staggered backward.

Harmony Vineyard. Ben eased the Chevy out of the parking lot into the street. "Awfully quiet. You okay?"

"No."

"What happened?"

"Well, he's not a bad guy. But that's worse."

"Meaning?"

"Good people are so sure about not being prejudiced. They don't listen. They don't see themselves."

Hogan Prep. The stadium seats were unforgiving, hard as church pews.

Parents cheered and hollered throughout the game, as though it were an ordinary day.

I'd reduced those young men to my racist expectations. When they'd given me directions, had shock registered on my face? I reeled at the possibility. I wailed at all the suspicion they endured. Wailed at the image of white ladies who stiffened their shoulders and clutched their purses at the approach of three black teens. How often did I clutch my purse?

"Goes out for the pass. He's at the thirty, the twenty. Knocked out of bounds."

Hogan Prep trounced our team.

My nephew would be inconsolable.

I climbed down from the stands, reluctant to face him, afraid he would see me as I really am.

THIRTY-ONE AMERICANS

An ambulance shriek closes in. From which direction? Where? Where? I slam on the brakes midway through a left turn, and the ambulance screams past, dangerously close to my front bumper. After traffic nudges back to life, I'm frozen for a second, trying to remember how to drive.

I've just come from the art museum. I'd gone solo, so the visual images could sink into my cells, unobstructed by conversation. *30 Americans*—an exhibit of American life, as interpreted by thirty contemporary black artists. It was a bad idea. Not the exhibit. My going to see the exhibit.

An engine revs; an SUV speeds by. Now I remember how to drive: Look both ways. Turn the steering wheel. Press the gas pedal. I cruise through the leafy neighborhood that surrounds the museum's manicured gardens. Several blocks ahead, the ambulance is shrinking, its siren receding.

I felt out of place among the white onlookers touring *30 Americans*, even though I was an onlooker, too, gawking at my own life. Four hundred years of color-infused emotions—mine, the artists', our ancestors'—

compressed into claustrophobic passageways and alcoves. I chuckled at a montage of our hair in its myriad configurations. Yup, I used to sport that stick-straight coif, thanks to a lye relaxer that—swear to god—I could still smell. And I fairly levitated with joy at a human-shaped sculpture made of flower blossoms. You couldn't identify gender, race, or age. Yes, let me see cabbage roses when I look at my enemies. Let the fragrance of gardenias hang in the air between us. Apparently, I have a greater capacity for despondence than optimism. Despite the intermittent uplift, four hundred years beat me down.

I pull up for a red light at a crossroad where high-end white Kansas City smacks up against low-end black Kansas City. Fast food. Bus stop. Cell phone mart. An urban apparel store sits across the street from a health clinic. Anchoring the corner is Walgreens, the place I stock up on eye shadow in shades designed for women of color.

The exhibition flowed into a corner housing an installation called "Duck, Duck, Noose." A circle of nine wooden stools. On each stool sat a KKK hood, empty eyeholes facing the center, where a rope dangled from the ceiling, the end pooled in tidy coils on the floor. I gasped. Run. Get the hell out of here. Stop looking. But "Duck, Duck, Noose" forced me to stare, like an assailant holding my head underwater. I stumbled past in a stupor.

The car in front of me sits a beat too long after the light turns green. Cell phone distraction? The driver creeps into the intersection. Stops again. What is he—?

In the fast food parking lot, the ambulance.

Two white policemen.

A black person flat on the ground. Face-up.

Bright flowered fabric across thighs. Skirt. A woman.

Still as a rock.

I clench the steering wheel. Hyperventilate. My vision blurs, and I realize I'm sobbing. Need to pull over, to park, to say oh my god, oh my god, but I can't remember how to stop driving. Automatic pilot glides the car past the scene, but my heart stumbles past it in a stupor.

On the highway, as grief makes a slick mess of my face, a slide show plays the images my brain has photographed. She's on her back, arms and legs spread. Her head is inches from the policemen's polished shoes. Her legs span the sidewalk. The patrolmen stand beside their car, hands resting on their heavy-laden belts. They appear to watch traffic go by. If she were alive, they'd be kneeling at her side, wouldn't they? They'd be making her comfortable, wouldn't they? The EMTs would be rushing to her aid, wouldn't they? There is an absence of urgency.

She's alone. May she find peace. Her family's going to get a bad phone call. May they find peace.

I grip the steering wheel hard, to squeeze life back into its proper shape. So I can buy makeup again at Walgreens.

Maybe she's part of an art installation. I want her to be an art installation.

She's lying in savasana—corpse pose. She's anonymous. I name her Grace. Who lies at the intersection of life and art. Thirty-one Americans.

SEDUCED

was alone in the center of a crowded room, the bulls-eye in a target.
This did not happen.
Not here.

Excited about attending a Kirtan for the first time, I crossed a parking lot from my air-conditioned car toward an air-conditioned yoga studio. The glass door snugged closed, freeing me from triple-digit heat. I paused to thank every Hindu deity I could imagine for relief from summer's oppression.

Long-time friend Victor had invited me to the Sanskrit chanting practice, at which he would play guitar and sing.

Tucking my shoes into a cubbyhole—a welcome bit of yoga ritual in a studio that was otherwise new to me—I grabbed a song sheet from a stack on a table and then slipped into the main room. Folding chairs had been arranged in tidy rows. I claimed a seat in the front row. A few women had already unfurled yoga mats and were sitting cross-leg-ged on the floor in front of the chairs. Others sprawled on cushions.

Beneath miniature white lights strung in lazy loops across the ceiling, the musicians were transforming one corner into a stage, arranging amplifiers, microphones, cords, and instruments. Instruments that Victor would later introduce like visiting dignitaries. *Mridanga*, a floor drum of southern India. *Tablas*, hand drums from the north by way of ancient Arabia. *Harmonium*, a keyboard originally from England.

Fay, the lead singer, played the harmonium. She directed our attention to a chant at the bottom of our song sheets, a call and response. Fay sang the call and Victor led the audience response. "*Hare Krishna. Hare Krishna. Krishna Krishna. Hare Hare.*" My voice at first uncertain, I grew more confident after every verse. "*Hare Rama. Hare Rama. Rama Rama. Hare Hare.*" Accentuated by the beat of tablas, the chant pulled me in with a promise of ascension … from the body … from the chair … from the earth.

The audience grew; our sparse numbers multiplied into a crowd. As latecomers slipped into the row behind me, their cotton shirts brushed the back of my neck. Except for me—the single African American in the studio—my row remained empty. I suspected a connection between those facts but turned away from suspicion toward the lure of transcendence.

Victor leaned into his mic. "If you're new to Kirtan, don't worry. Join in. Dance, if the music moves you. Soak up the energy."

I glanced at the typewritten page on my lap, lifted my voice in adoration, and soaked up the energy.

After exalting Lord Krishna, we called on the goddesses. Fay's soprano shimmered. The divine feminine beckoned. We followed. We appealed to the goddess of art and creativity. "*He Saraswati.*" The goddess of prosperity and wealth. "*He Maha Lakshmi.*" The goddess of transformation and death. "*He Mata Kali.*" I came to them like a child. "*Jagatambe Jai Jai Ma. Jagatambe Jai Jai Ma.*" They smothered me with kisses.

Incense sweetened the air. Fingers of smoke curled in ever-shifting directions as new arrivals trickled in. A man and woman grabbed chairs at the opposite end of my row and scooted them farther away, as if positioning for a better view, even though the people in front were on the floor. Sitting at one end of a long empty row, I felt like a single person on a teeter-totter.

Sanskrit made me tongue-tied, but the next chant began slowly enough for me to pick up pronunciations. *Om* terra. *Too*-terra. Too-*ray*. So-*hah*. Syllables popped from my throat; I was the drum. "*Om* terra. *Too*-terra." I rocked from side to side. "Too-*ray*. So-*hah*." The chant sped up. "*Om* terra. *Too*-terra. Too-*ray*. So-*hah*." Rhythm captured my feet. "*Om* terra. *Too*-terra. Too-*ray*. So-*hah*." I welcomed oblivion. Shatter me. Blast the shards to the winds. I wasn't singing any longer, only sputtering guttural noises, desperate for Tara to take me, my voice giving out for lack of breath, and as the percussionist pounded a final thunderclap, Victor swung his guitar over his head and mimed smashing it onto the stage. Praise God!

Fay rose from her seat at the harmonium and knelt on the floor, crystal bowls lined up at her knees. "We'll slow the energy down a bit, so you can drive home safely." She swiped a wooden stick around the rims of the bowls and began the closing chant. I was disappointed the lyrics were in English, which normally triggered my intellect to spring into analysis and debate. By this point in the evening, though, my mind had surrendered. After rounds of "Peace across the land and in the deep blue sea," a longing for peace trickled down my cheeks in rivulets. My voice shook. I could only mouth the final words. A deep tone from the largest crystal bowl lingered … melted away …

The musicians bowed. I lowered my head. "Namaste."

Eyes closed, I waited for my emotions to settle and for the rustle of an audience preparing to leave. But instead of *goodnight, thank you for coming*, Fay announced, "We're going to end with a ritual to honor the light in each of us. Choose a partner and stand facing each other."

Still in a fog, I rose from my chair. Waves of motion rippled across the room, as chairs and cushions were pushed aside. There was a milling around, the chatter of voices, the slip and pad of bare feet. Pairs sprouted along the walls and in the corners. Twos expanded into fours and then sixes, which whorled around the studio, filling in the empty spaces. The figures were ghostly, floating in incense clouds and the half-light of a setting sun. When the mingling slowed to a standstill, and the chatter tapered off to murmur, and the choosing was complete—

I was alone in the center of the room.

The bulls-eye in a target.

This did not happen.

Not here.

Of course it happened.

Here.

I should have seen it coming.

Stupid, stupid woman. To be seduced by the possibility of love in a room full of white people was as reckless as mooning over a married man.

I fought the urge to run. Fleeing would draw attention. The only thing that would save me from humiliation was the invisibility that had caused it. That, and hatred. My eyes narrowed to slits, my cheeks flushed hot, I coiled, ready to savage this roomful of devotees. My fists gnarled into witch's hands with hooked nails to tear bloody stripes across the backs these worshipers had turned on me, to rip all those pink feet from their shocked ankles—feet that walked away from me and danced to the beat of God's lying heart.

A command from the stage startled my hatred. "You two pair up."

Fay was spotlighted under the twinkling lights, one hand pointed at a woman on the far side of the studio, the other at me. The woman hurried toward me.

Like Gollum, malice retreated into its cave, which allowed my eye slits to open in welcome.

Just get through it, Dawn.

Nose to nose with our partners, we formed two concentric circles. Those on the inside faced out, those on the outside faced in. Music swelled; we sang a verse; the outer circle shifted to the right. I was opposite a different partner. We chanted and bowed. Singing into those other eyes, I was looking into faces of innocence, moonlit orbs that reflected *namasté*. We were unspoiled. We were pure of motive, every one of us. When the light in me bowed to the light in each of my partners, my personality, wearing its crown of slights, dissolved.

Soon enough the exercise ended. Regulars exploded out of their reverie into gossipy groups, and still I expected someone to offer an outstretched hand in welcome. Or apology. None did.

I threaded through knots of well-wishers to compliment the musicians. Victor was stuffing cords into a plastic bin. I hoped he hadn't noticed me un-chosen in the middle of the room, and also hoped he had. We hugged and laughed, my *hello, that was wonderful* followed by his *so glad you were here, thanks for coming*. His effervescence seemed an indication he had not noticed. My good cheer, on the other hand, was a nervous tic. Our words swallowed by the surrounding din, I turned away, intending to say hello to Fay. I hoped for a remorseful acknowledgement of the scene she'd witnessed, which would reverse the last hour back to the promise of "*Hare Krishna. Krishna. Krishna.*" But she was deep in conversation.

My feet stuck to the floor. Go? Stay? I was rickety, nailed together with mismatched emotions.

I stumbled away, reclaimed my shoes, and opened the door to leave the studio. The summer night seared my face—heat so oppressive I couldn't breathe.

LIZA AND ME

The drawer of the DVD player slides into place, closing the door on the stresses and strains of my day. A recliner embraces my world-weary muscles, as I flip the handle on the side and pop up the footrest. I snuggle under a blanket, a crockery bowl of still-warm popcorn in the crook of my arm. Movie time. Across the television screen, opening credits announce *Liza with a Z*, a 1972 song-and-dance television special. The star and her chorus line are probably coiled just off stage, anticipating their cue.

I know that feeling.

At twelve, I tagged along when my parents took my big sister to audition for *The Pirates of Penzance*. After Big Sis finished, the pianist turned to me. "You're up next."

"Huh?"

My step-mom pushed me forward, in that parental way that makes it clear you have no choice. After I do-re-me'd and fa-la-la'd for the pianist, he nodded. "Okay, you're in."

I didn't even know what *in* meant.

I was cast in the chorus.

Theatre people were witty and chatty. They were the in-crowd, and I was one of them. They performed nightly miracles for this lonely pre-teen. Costume fittings made me look beautiful. Rehearsals made me sound beautiful. Curtain calls made me feel beautiful. For the first time in my scrawny, scared-of-my-shadow (and yours, too) life, I let down my guard.

Every night, we daughters of the major general posed behind the curtain, positioned for our entrance. Every night, a *Penzance* sister would give me a thumbs-up.

Liza and me. Waiting for our cues.

I crunch a mouthful of popcorn and tuck in the blanket to ward off a draft. On the television screen, dancers inch sideways across the boards, in top hats and tails—knees and toes turned in, then out, then in again. Fingers splayed, alternately hunching and rolling their shoulders. Signature Bob Fosse choreography. Liza's probably warming up backstage, an image that shoots a jolt of happy through my toes. I windshield wiper my feet in place. They want to dance.

In college, modern dance was the only class I showed up for on a regular basis. Every time I crossed the threshold, the studio welcomed my bare feet back home. I padded over to my place, the floor an expanse of wood warmed by sun pouring in through a skylight. Like the other girls, I wore a brightly colored leotard and footless tights, leg warmers bunched around my ankles. We were in uniform, right down to our sweatbands—mine holding back my Afro. One after another, we glided past our instructor, our parade reflected in floor-to-ceiling mirrors. I admired the graceful arc each of us carved, as she swirled on command, head tilted and outstretched arms curved ever so slightly. Under the studio's beamed ceiling, shyness lifted. I watched the other girls. They watched me.

Liza and me. Dancers.

Snug beneath my blanket, I anticipate my hero's entrance. The only thing better than sexy Bob Fosse choreography is Liza Minnelli performing it. She slinks on from stage right, squeezed shoulder to shoulder with the others in the front row, her precision movements identical to theirs. She's just another cog in the machinery. Except—against a corps of tuxedo-clad hoofers, Liza sports a red mini-dress. The dress makes love to her curves from squared shoulders, past nipped waistline, to a stopping point just below her bottom. I'm worried an inadvertent kick will reveal her underwear. I'm a little titillated too; no matter how high she kicks, her undies never show, and I kind of wish they did. God, that dress is short.

Back in 1972, a red mini hung in my dorm room closet. According to my best friend, the dress spent more time on the dance floor than in the closet. A sleeveless bodice cinched my waist and was attached to a gathered skirt, which draped modestly to my knees. Well, it had draped modestly to my knees at the time Mother had bought it for me. After I went off to college, I shortened the demure frock to barely past don't-bend-over. In street clothes, I shuffled, tripped, and kept my head down, but when I slipped into that little red come-hither—Lord have mercy. In smoky party rooms, pounding bass pumped up my nerve, igniting my signature shoulder pump. As I thrust and spun to the throb of disco, silk swished against my hips. God, that dress was short.

Liza and me. Red-dress flirts.

Between numbers, Minnelli shares stories with the audience, a bowler hat tilted to set off her fake lashes. Her demeanor slides from sexy to demure and back again. Wide-eyed innocence and breathy inflection—the spitting image of her mother, Judy Garland. Any minute, I expect the *Cabaret* star to start calling for Auntie Em. Which makes me weepy, like the time Uncle Al told me, "You're the spittin' image of Catherine." My mama. His proclamation had validated my membership in our tribe. He'd handed me a ticket to belonging.

Liza and me. Carbon copies of our mamas.

Liza grew up on movie sets. Her mother performed in musicals directed by her father, Vincent Minnelli. The last one, *Till the Clouds Roll By*, came out the year Liza was born. Judy Garland might have been pregnant at that premier, walking the red carpet in a sparkly maternity outfit. When Liza was three, she had a cameo in Garland's movie, *In the Good Old Summertime*; and an old photo shows four-year-old Liza posed at her mother's side on the set of *Summer Stock*. Liza's younger sister Lorna debuted at eleven, she and Liza singing Christmas carols on television's *The Judy Garland Show*. Lorna built a musical theatre career, and Liza's brother Joey Luft was also a singer.

I grew up backstage. Dad was an actor and teacher from the time I took my first bow in *Pirates of Penzance*. After Big Sis's lead role in *Penzance*, she became a professional singer, who performed all around the country and Scotland, too. My brother and uncle became actors who earned movie credits—my brother also a director, producer, and drama professor. I basked in their reflected glory, a celebrity because I was somebody's daughter, sister, and niece. The performance bug bit me late in life, transforming my hometown book reading into a Broadway production, me center stage as star and scriptwriter, my sister singing, my niece acting, and my brother producing and directing.

Liza and me. Show-biz sisters.

—◦—

The television flickers. As I shift to find the sweet spot, the recliner gives a bit, in recognition of its important role in our shared hour of bliss. Liza twirls across the stage, all the while her singing voice as nimble as her body. I want to leap up, dance straight to the current writing project waiting on the laptop, certain the essay will become a critically acclaimed memoir. My idol's performance proves everything's possible, if I'm willing to work my butt off. She's made it big with her creativity; I can make it big with mine. I'm mesmerized by her razzle-dazzle and high on buttery popcorn fumes, but writing will have to wait. I'm sticking with Liza till the end of her show.

The outside world does a slow dissolve, while I tap out show tunes against the arm of the chair. There's only the music, the dancers, and me.

A costume change puts our headliner in knickers and tights, straight out of Charles Dickens. A weird outfit, but hey, the seventies were not known for classic fashion. And, damn, Liza pulls it off. The stage darkens to a fuzzy spotlight. She shakes her head, ruffles her hair. When she looks up again, she smiles at me, her features melancholy. Wow. She rearranges the molecules in her face to catch every fleeting mood. She oozes into a ballad, low and mournful. I snuggle under my blankey.

As the piano moans minor chords, I turn to mush in sympathy for those eyes, sad as a lost puppy's.

The wistful camera moves in for a close-up of her porcelain cheek and slicked-down sideburn. Her eyes are moist, her voice honey. "Mammy ..."

My jaw drops open mid-chew.

What?

Did she say *mammy*? I squint at the television, because you can hear better when you squint. My ears are convinced by the dreamy music, and my heart can't help responding when she bats those lashes, heavy with loss and—

"My mammy …"

She did say *mammy*. My gut clenches, but I refuse to believe the message being telegraphed. Surely, my gut doesn't know anything about Liza's intention. Any second she'll reveal the song is a joke. She's making fun of minstrel shows. This is a sophisticated New York City satire. I command my body to stay in neutral until all the evidence is—

"Alabammy …"

Liza Minnelli in black knickers turns into Al Jolson in blackface.

I hurl the bowl at her face, leap from the chair, and slam the television onto the floor. "I hate you!" Smashing glass rings in my ears, as I stomp the shattered screen to bits.

In my mind, that's what happens.

In reality, I sag. Limp as the blanket. Gaping at the traitorous television, as popcorn dribbles out of my hand. My soul floats out the window to safety, leaving behind a shell of Dawn-shaped skin.

The tune speeds toward conclusion. Liza drops to one knee, belting out the final notes, arms wide. "… my ma - a- a - me-ee!"

A thunderous ovation follows her bow.

I trusted her. She's my show biz sister. She loved me.

Liza …?

… and me?

God, even Mother—my white stepmom—had fantasized herself as Scarlett O'Hara. Had the fantasy included being clucked over by a shoe-shine-black, bandana-wearing slave, like Scarlett's Mammy? "I says I gwine with you … and gwine I is!"

Liza flashes a crooked Judy Garland grin. I'm nauseous. Did Judy Garland sing *My Mammy*? Did the daughter inherit the song, as Scarlett inherited the slave?

I cannot reason out why Liza's waxing lyrical about her mammy in Alabammy, Southern California being the farthest south she's ever lived. Born to Hollywood royalty. Spent her childhood on movie sets. Grew up to become a quintessential New Yorker. I assumed a cultural sophistication to match her edgy haircut.

The television's flickering images mock me. They know what will follow: friends will tell me it's just a song; Liza didn't mean anything. Of course it's just a song. I'm a deleted verse. Of course she doesn't mean anything. I don't mean anything. Friends will expect me to remain a faithful fan. My dancing feet say yes, a fan forever. My gut says hell no.

My bottom lip stiffens as I sink into suspended animation, blindsided by the myth of myself as human.

Look at Liza, taking her bow, gazing into the camera. Affection shining through her eyes.

Liza and me.

We dance. Me, hopping to the snap of a whip.

We wear red. Me, sporting a bandana over shameful naps.

We act. Me, delivering the expected line: *Chile, dat sho nuff a purty song.*

Liza and me. White girl and mammy.

PART TWO

FINAL REPORT OF THE
DAWN DOWNEY DIVERSITY COMMITTEE

Kansas City, MO
January 13, 2020

Report commissioned by: Dawn Downey, CEO of DD Inc.
Diversity Committee Members:
Dawn Downey, Blogger
Dawn Downey, Lifestyle Critic
Dawn Downey, Accountant
Dawn Downey, Readers' Representative
Implementation assigned to: Dawn Downey, Public Relations Director for DD Inc.

This Report follows an investigation launched after Concerned Citizen Dawn Downey lodged an official complaint with the Dawn Downey Diversity Committee: Complaint #159, dated November 1, 2019. The Complainant (Dawn Downey) alleges that Author Dawn Downey practices and perpetuates segregation inside the Dawn Downey Friendship Circle. In fact, the Complainant alleges Author Dawn Downey has become color-blind, that is to say, her sight has been blinded by the whiteness of her Friendship Circle.

We note Author DD's numerous claims of being victimized by Race-Related Microaggressions (see subsection 743a "Seduced" and subsection 858c "Comfort Food"). The Complainant alleges, due to Author DD's systemic discrimination against Women of Color, Author DD's claims to victimhood lack credibility.

THE FACTS

- Author DD's Facebook Friends list. 97% white. 3% Downey.

- Author DD is the only non-white person in attendance at her book readings.

- Author DD resides in a white suburban neighborhood, the establishment of said neighborhood having historical roots in white flight.

- Author DD claims in sworn video testimony, "No, really, my best friend is from the hood." However, when pressed for details, she states the residence of her alleged Black Best Friend is "Los Angeles … maybe Memphis," and the frequency of phone calls between them is "every couple of years, but it's like no time has passed." We are outraged by this thinly-veiled attempt to deceive the Committee.

SYSTEMIC BARRIERS TO ACCESS

- No workplace affiliation. Women of Color cannot connect in person with DD through her job site, because her place of work is her computer. In her bedroom.

- No professional peer group affiliation. Women of Color represent a significant portion of the population of her professional peer group (i.e. Writers), but they are hunkered down at their own computers in their own bedrooms.

- No church affiliation. Although DD has attended religious ceremonies across the ethnic spectrum, the Committee finds that her repeated tirades against "some supernatural overlord calling the shots" (her words, not ours) make her an unlikely candidate for church-related friendships.

- No beauty shop affiliation. DD has her hair cut by a white stylist. The Committee feels this is particularly appalling and cannot accept Author DD's justification that the stylist prominently displays a life-sized photo of Tina Turner.
- No geographically feasible family affiliation. DD lives 7,000,000.4 miles from her family, and even if she lived closer—most of their friends are white, too.

RECOMMENDED AFFIRMATIVE ACTION STRATEGIES

- Recruitment. Set up a booth at Powwows and Day of the Dead Festivals, under the banner: "Imagine the Possibilities—Reclusive Writer as Your BFF!" (According to security footage from a writers' conference, Author DD followed a Cherokee author from registration to workshops, to lunch, and into a restroom, where Author DD begged Ms. Cherokee Author, "Will you please be my friend?" The Diversity Committee regards this strategy as antithetical to achieving diversity goals.)
- Ethnic Girlfriend Month. Write essays every April, imagining the potential friendships of famous Women of Color, such as Frida Kahlo and Queen Nefertiti.
- Reparations. Make direct payments to Women of Color (and their descendants) who were excluded from the Dawn Downey Friendship Circle between the years 2017 and 2020. This covers the time period during which she was writing *Blindsided: Essays from the Only Black Woman in the Room*. The Diversity Committee is adamant Downey should not profit from the immoral condition that she herself created.
- Web presence. Establish a social media site (Me-Neither.com) where Women of Color share their personal stories about not being friends with Author DD.

- Bussing. Chauffeur Women of Color to and from all book readings.
- Free Lunch Program. Buy lunch every week for a year for Women of Color who accept membership in the Dawn Downey Friendship Circle.
- Quotas. Set aside 25% of all new Friendship positions for Women of Color.
- Nepotism. Award immediate Friendship status to any Woman of Color related to DD through blood or marriage.

In Conclusion

- The Investigation substantiates the allegation that, due to Author Dawn Downey's color-blindness, Women of Color represent an inadequate percentage (0.0%) of the Dawn Downey Friendship Circle.
- The Diversity Committee urges Author DD to immediately implement the Affirmative Action Strategies outlined in the Report.
- Following implementation of the Strategies, The Committee will permit Author Dawn Downey to resume writing stories about Race-Related Microaggressions. However, such permission does not guarantee protection from future occurrences of said R-RMs. Additional action may be required (see subsection 985d: "The Race Card.")
- The Committee cautions Author DD against relegating The Report to the status of previous Diversity Committee Reports, which are currently shelved in the Affirmative Action Strategies Archives Library Sub-basement.

THE CLEANING WOMEN

My question required sidling up to, the way a maid would ask for a day off. The conversation would be chancy with the white women milling around the yoga studio putting away their props. I could not risk the word *housekeeper*—colored girls in head rags crowded in on the word, mopping, scrubbing, and taking home leftovers. If I broached the subject head-on, these friends-for-now would know by the set of my mouth that I'd been on hands and knees on a white woman's kitchen floor. Their expressions would suggest that was the proper order of things.

Pottery Barn catalog in hand, I sagged onto my couch and propped my feet up on the coffee table. When I pushed aside a star-shaped basket, it left a five-pointed dust-free spot. I looked away, but a cobweb strand denounced me, dangling from the middle of the ceiling to a yoga mat unfurled on the floor. Crumbs reproached my bare feet, and the odor of last night's fish-fry skillet indicted my nose.

Get off your lazy butt and clean this place.

I dropped the catalog. Who was I to own monogrammed sheets? Linen napkins would refuse delivery to my address. Silk throw pillows would insist the UPS driver take them up the hill where rich women hired help.

In the 1940s my grandmother Mon (she'd have me tell you the nickname rhymes with sun) cleaned for white ladies. She spoke of them in fondness and gave up housework only when a better job came along: high school custodian. Better, because it included a pension, and the paychecks were regular.

My Mon, a janitor? She owned a grand piano. Polished to a blinding shine, it held court in her formal living room—not to be confused with her informal sitting room just off the front porch. Mon's long brown fingers flew over the keys as she taught me to play "Clair de Lune." A ruby-hued velvet couch, its back a graceful curve, sat against one wall. An expanse of fleur-de-lis-patterned carpet swept across the room to matching chairs on the far side.

My grandmother, a maid? She owned two sets of flatware. Stainless steel in the drawer for everyday, and silver stored inside a wooden chest for Easter and Christmas. Her closets were stuffed with pretty things. Orderly rows of dresses, ankle-strap high heels along the floor, and a fox wrap draped around a hanger.

My grandmother? Scrubbed toilets? Glass bricks formed a wall behind a breakfast nook in her kitchen. When I was a little girl I sat there watching dappled sunlight play on the table and crunching bacon strips she'd set on my plate. She would rest the skillet on an iron trivet—one of a dozen that appeared whenever a hot pan threatened a counter. And on her screened-in front porch, an apple green glider that I set in motion with my big toe, while wind chimes sang to me like angels.

Weekends at Mon's house were a respite from real life.

Real life lived in Mama's house. No glider on our front porch. Instead: peeling paint, squeaky floorboards, and a razor strop, which hung in the vestibule. In real life, the kitchen floor was stamped with footprints ground in by muddy boots. In real life, Mama scuffed around in a shapeless housedress and used-to-be-pink slippers.

Our golden retriever lived in the basement, and even though my brother shoveled droppings off the concrete floor every day, he could never shovel away the stink. When Mama cooked chitlins, the stench clung to walls and furniture and the back of my throat. The smell was almost as bad on the days she boiled mustard greens.

On one of those mustard-greens days, while I was playing on my bedroom floor, a dark shape, antenna waving, inched up the inside of my blouse. I screamed, batted at my chest, tore off the blouse, and flung it across the room. I stomped a wad of covers that had fallen off the bed, in case more roaches were hiding in the folds. With all the strength in my skinny arm, I hurled a shoe at the window. The crash of shattering glass was both a shock and a balm. Why couldn't I live at Mon's?

I was in high school, living with Dad halfway across the country, when I learned Mama cleaned houses too. She rode the bus to and from the suburbs, squeezed in among the other help. I learned it in the nebulous way that family stories enter one's consciousness. I knew Mama cleaned for white ladies, but didn't want to know it. Especially since I found out she was a maid during the same year I learned the provenance of Mon's silver. The set in the pretty wooden box had been a cast-off from one of the women Mon had cleaned for. *Give the dull knives to the colored woman, or toss them in the trash. Makes no difference.*

When I realized the truth about Mon's silver, my admiration crusted over into shame.

But by then—the high school years—self-hatred was already crawling up my skin like a roach. *Not good enough* caused me to be reserved, which the girls at my new school mistook for haughtiness. Black girls called me a high yellow bitch. Perhaps I had begun turning inward earlier, at fourteen, in American history class. On the day we studied slavery, attention had leaned in my direction, the other students sneaking a peek at the Negro. While the teacher had droned on about half-naked girls on the auction block, I'd felt the sideways eyes of my classmates determining my price.

~∞~

After taking an early retirement, I worked part-time assisting seniors who lived independently. One of my clients needed help tidying up her tiny apartment, a mindless chore that appealed to me after decades of climbing the corporate ladder. I liked this soft-spoken white woman the instant she invited me in, with a wave of her hand and an offer of candy from a dish on the coffee table. Such a grandma thing to do. She explained the only way to clean floors was on all fours, an opinion my own experience validated; but as soon as my knees hit the tile, I was seething. *You've got a master's degree, Dawn. What the hell are you doing on this woman's kitchen floor?* I wanted nothing more than to strangle this sweet grandma, and the women who'd given my grandmother gifts, and the women who'd hired my mother, and every other white woman who'd hired help.

~∞~

I picked up the Pottery Barn catalog and dropped it into the recycle bin in the kitchen. My weariness ground footprints into the linoleum, and the footprints led to shame, and the shame circled back to weariness, which led to chitlins stinking up my peace of mind.

I wanted to live in a house like Mon's, but Mama's was the one I deserved.

After my want nudged past my inadequacy, I Googled "cleaning services in Kansas City." Sifting through the list turned out to be one more chore too big for me to start.

The search had to be narrowed. I'd have to ask someone. The women in my writers' group lived in apartments. My book group? The same.

Yoga? My age. Homeowners. A few had grown into what I dared label friends. How long would that last if any of them had actually hired a housekeeper … although nobody used that word anymore. Well then, if they'd hired a cleaning service. If they were that well off … although one was a policeman's wife, and another lived in a house smaller than mine, and another was paying for her mother's nursing home. None of them were rich. Still … it would be risky to talk to white women about cleaning houses, and if they recommended their cleaning service …

Jesus, don't let them say, "You'll love her."

Like the acquaintance who had been excited to introduce me to an artist he'd discovered. "Such an inspiration. You'll love him." Like the colleague who'd recommended an author. "Reminds me of you. You'll love her." Thrilled, foolish, each time I clicked the mentioned website. The artist was black. The author, too. And I was the black writer-friend. I waited for the next betrayal.

Four of us straggled after yoga class, always the same four, unwilling to leave each other's company just yet. My lingering was mixed with hesitation, while I waited for a wisp of courage.

I rolled my mat a turn. "Lynn, you teach all day …" I patted the edges even. "… yard's gorgeous." I rolled another turn. "How do you keep up your house?"

"Don't," she said.

Dee shoved a bolster into the corner. "Me neither."

Marilyn was at the check-in desk, flipping through an index file, looking for the card that bore her name. "Clean house? Give up my two-hour walks? Oh, hell, no. I deserve time for myself."

I chuckled, pretending to understand *I deserve.*

In the language of my upbringing, words that followed *deserve* were: *to be taken down a notch.* Or: *a good smack.* Or: *a week in your room.* While the syllables were arranging themselves into words, and the words were lining up into a comprehensible sentence, Dee said, "I don't feel like it anymore."

I could not imagine uttering those words.

Weekends at Mon's, I had made my bed in the morning and put toys away before supper. If you didn't feel like putting the toys away, she didn't feel like letting you play with them again. Did she have feelings about cleaning her house? There were no dirty dishes after she fixed my bacon. The Steinway always gleamed, bench slid underneath, sheet music tucked inside. *The Ottumwa Courier* was the only item allowed out of place, tossed on the foot of her daybed after she worked the crossword puzzle.

Atop a pyramid of rolled-up mats in the corner, I carefully added mine. "Dee, your house is spotless. Mine's a mess."

She and Marilyn said, "Sarah."

I waited for *you'll love her.*

My apprehension drowned out most of the conversation. Snippets sneaked in. "Knows about birds." "Goes to yoga." "Like being around her."

I gulped. "How often does she come?"

"Set your own schedule."

Hire help. Set the schedule. The power was heady, yet fraught with hazard. Let a stranger into my space, which was so cluttered with self-criticism?

Dee plucked her phone from her purse. "I'm texting you her number."

Sarah came by to work out an estimate. I opened the door to greet her, and my shoulders eased when I saw she was white. I studied her face for any slight raise of an eyebrow that would betray hesitation at cleaning a black woman's house.

She had eyes only for the work. She studied grime with a professional detachment—her pace deliberate through the kitchen, bedrooms, and bathrooms. As though wearing white gloves, she brushed the frame of a Van Gogh print above my bed. "I'll dust the tops of picture frames for you." *Starry Night* had long ago disappeared from my awareness, but it could not hide from Sarah. It was harboring her enemy—dirt. She paused in the hallway to admire a Tibetan thangka. "Pretty wall hanging."

I tagged along behind her, a little girl who'd just acquired a fairy godmother. Happy energy swirled in her wake like fireflies around the hem of her gown. Windows were magically thrown open as she passed. Dust bunnies hopped away smiling.

Her presence was a cross breeze airing out my musty insecurities.

Back in the kitchen, she glanced into the back yard. "See that little bird out by your fence? It's a junco. He'll poke around under your feeder if you sprinkle sunflower seeds on the ground."

We agreed on a price and then scheduled the job. Mon's trivets, hanging on the wall above my stove, supervised the transaction.

Sarah hugged me goodbye. "Gotta go do my house now."

Clean mine. Clean hers. It was all the same to her, a task to be checked off her list. A client to be added to her customer base. "See you next week."

A white woman was going to clean my house. Mon and Mama chuckled at the notion. Their white ladies chuckled too, because I had hired help—just as they had. My yoga classmates would chuckle in bemusement that *help* was anything other than a solution to a problem. What's the fuss? Dirty house? Call Sarah.

I brushed the nap of my velvet couch. Discovered in an antique store, it might have been a shoestring relative of Mon's sofa, which she had bought with money earned from housework. A cobweb sneaked across the baseboard (Sarah would make short work of it). Relaxing in a rocking chair, I wondered if Mama and Mon would have wished for fairy godmothers, too. My big toe set the chair in motion—the rhythmic squeak of floorboards like an angel's song. Sarah hadn't asked where I'd gotten the Tibetan thangka she'd admired. She'd acted as though its hanging there were perfectly normal. As if I deserved my pretty things.

THE RACE CARD

I wait for Ben to join me inside the hardware store. He's returned to the car for his phone. We need our phones, because I tend to wander off while shopping. That, combined with my absent-mindedness, presents potential for trouble. Once, not paying attention, I'd almost stuck my hand into the back pocket of a short round white guy, mistaking him for the short round white guy I'm married to.

The store's entry is more spacious than I'd expect, as big as a cineplex lobby. How fitting they've set up a section of munchies right by the door, like a concession stand. For a movie fan/hardware nerd like me, this has just become an ideal entertainment venue. I grab myself a bag of Cheetos.

There are two cashiers in sight; one of them is either asleep or in a coma. The other, a middle-aged man, is engrossed in a magazine, but sees me through the eyes in the back of his head. He scans the Cheeto bag and turns pages simultaneously. "Dollar seventy-three," he says to his magazine, then shoves the cash into the drawer. "Want your receipt?" he asks the cash register.

On behalf of the register, I say, "No thanks."

I forgive this level of surliness in teenaged clerks. They've earned the right to a bad attitude, given the hormones wreaking havoc in their systems. But from a man old enough to shoulder a mortgage,

I'm accustomed to some attention, even if only a sexist, *Have a good day, little lady.* The cashier's hostility puts me on edge.

I shake off the mood. Lousy service will not be allowed to ruin my Tuesday with Ben. After you've been married a long time, you have to treat every outing like a date. Hold hands, sing show tunes, talk in married-people code. When he comes in, I offer hubby a Cheeto.

"No thanks," he says. "I'm going for the free popcorn over here."

Free popcorn? I love this place. After filling up at the popcorn station, we meander to housewares, on the hunt for picture hooks. No hooks in sight, but they do have a spiffy pop-open laundry hamper, which I snatch up.

We examine a red wagon and some bicycle tires. Total browsing satisfaction awaits over in automotive, plumbing, and possibly electrical supplies. Nothing beats a Cheeto-crunching tour of electrical—

"Hello?" A sales associate has materialized at the end of a long aisle. Mr. Coma. All stretched out and vertical, he's very tall, but awkward. He must have had a growth spurt in his teens that he never got used to. He creeps forward a step or two. Reluctant, like he's sneaking up on himself. I sense stalker vibrations. Has he been following us? "Hello?"

All too frequently, that same greeting had floated my way across a tony department store. The scenario had played out with eerie consistency. First, I'd get stalker shivers, then an apparition would appear in my peripheral vision, followed by the realization that said apparition had haunted my route from lingerie to jewelry to shoes. "Hello?" The unspoken questions trailing like cigar smoke: *Are you lost? You didn't use our restroom, did you? May I direct you back to the ghetto?* After surveilling too many customers, the tony department store had found itself on the losing end of a civil rights lawsuit.

Maybe Mr. Coma is talking to someone else. I check behind me. A matching white couple is wandering around the pet supplies section. Ben and I are the only customers facing the associate. I refuse to acknowledge the hello.

Ben says, "Hi, we're looking for hooks."

"Third aisle over, on your left."

I spot them immediately, exactly what I need. I admire any employee who knows his inventory. Triumphant and grateful, I wave at Mr. Coma, who's reappeared, peeking through a row of cleaning buckets. "Perfect. Thank you."

To the left of me, my husband also says, "Thanks."

Mr. Coma looks to my left. "You're welcome."

I crush the Cheeto I'm about to pop in my mouth, yellow paste bleeding all over my fingers. There's nothing more infuriating than wasting a peace offering on an enemy who ignores your existence. After smearing the Cheeto paste on the inside of my jeans pocket, I hurl the crumpled bag into a trash can.

We circle around to the paint section, pick up a bottle of mineral oil, and then head for checkout, where the magazine-reading cashier is still engrossed. As Ben drops the first item onto the counter, the cashier leaps to attention and beams. "Morning, sir. Find everything you need?"

Jerk. My face hardens into battle mode, but an explosion will blindside Ben, whose good cheer tells me he's oblivious to this war. It will be better for our marriage to stay calm for now and tell him my story after we get home.

Our loot disappears into a plastic sack. Hating the plastic, hating the cashier, I remove our loot, dropping the bag like a dirty diaper. "You can keep your bag."

Re-absorbed in his magazine, the cashier snatches the plastic off the counter, wads it up, and jams it into the trash. The eyes in the back of his head glare at me.

Screw marital harmony.

I unsheathe my Negress spear, raise it overhead, and prepare to plunge it through the cashier's heart. I am stopped mid-stab by an epiphany.

Existence inside a Negress skin just doesn't work for me anymore. Every morning, I wake up trapped in a relentless slog. Half the time suppressing a low-grade dread coiled at the base of my brain stem. The other half suppressing the urge to scream. Black comes without vacation days. No weekends off. No hope of retirement. I quit.

I will stop being colored.

Content with my non-violent solution (wouldn't Dr. King be proud of me?), I sheathe my spear. We gather our treasures and leave the store. Ben opens the car door for me. "There you go, darlin'." Our married-people date is saved.

I will stop being Negro.

On the drive home, I flesh out my plan. Strangers will need a warning, since they'll have no way of knowing about my change in status. Hmm ... something to prevent unfortunate interactions based on outdated information.

Introducing The Race Card. Customized notes to be distributed as follows:

Dear cashier: It's okay to make eye contact. I'm not black.

Dear sales associate: It's okay to not follow me around the store. I'm not black.

Dear neighbor: It's okay to skip asking me if I live around here. I'm not black.

Dear restaurant hostess: It's okay to seat me near the front door instead of the kitchen door. I'm not black.

Dear contractor: It's okay to repair my stoop. I'm not black.

Dear traffic cop: It's okay to forgo the speeding ticket for five miles over. I'm not black.

Dear conference attendee: It's okay to sit beside me. I'm not black.

Dear church-goer: It's okay to stop peeking. I'm not black.

Dear ally: It's okay to admit that all your friends are white. I'm not black.

Dear girlfriend: Its okay to love your own damn hair. I'm not black.

Dear funny guy: It's okay to say you *did* mean it that way. I'm not black.

And for occasions not otherwise specified, the general purpose race card. Dear citizen: It's okay to treat me like a run-of-the-mill Cheeto-lovin' earthling. I'm not black.

IDENTITY CRISIS: A TRIPTYCH

I

My cousins, siblings, and I were piled into Uncle Al's and Aunt Ruth's condo for a birthday party. From a couch, brother Michael, official Downey griot, recited family history, his snowy Afro and beard a halo around his California brown face. Another brother and my uncle squeezed in hip to hip beside him. Aunt Ruth, official Downey videographer, was planted in her usual spot, in an armchair. A side table held her tablet on the rare occasions when she set it down. There was spillover around the dining room table, and cousin Sherry and I were perched on bar stools.

Conversations criss-crossed mid-air. Uncle Al: "Best production the Playhouse ever did." Sherry: "You know his wife just got out of jail." Michael: "… and Mama's mother was white."

What—?

Aunt Ruth caught me open-mouthed.

Back up. Rewind. Do-over.

White?

Judging from the overwhelming non-reaction in the room— "Not half as good as *Kiss Me Kate*." "No, she got out last month."— the information was common knowledge. You'd think Michael had only said Mama's mother was short.

My maternal grandmother had died when I was a toddler. No photos survived. If Grandma had been white, what did that make me?

Was I too white to be black?

Will a congressional subcommittee take back all those Affirmative Action prizes, like my college education? Do I forfeit the title of First Black Girl at Santa Barbara High School to Wear an Afro? Should I inform my white husband our marriage is no longer interracial? Need I rescind my edginess at being the only black person in book group, yoga class, grocery line, craft fair, gallery opening, retreat center, hiking trail, IKEA store?

Ignorant of my own ethnicity, I cornered Michael in the kitchen, where no one else could hear. "You said Mama's mother was white?"

"No," he said. "Mama's *grand*mother was white."

Oh.

Never mind.

Still black.

Keeping the swag.

II

My family gathered to celebrate our patriarch's birthday. Aside from grandchildren and spouses, we were cousins who'd spent childhood walking-distance apart. Because black folk addressed me by names other than Dawn— High Yellow, Piss Colored, House Nigger—I tensed up around any of my people who were darker than me. I was fair game, and the next assault could come from anywhere. I set my face to neutral, although years had passed since one of my cousins had hurled *house nigger* at me. What's the matter, can't take a joke?

Amid reminders to "Keep it down; the neighbors can hear," family stories were shouted, debated, and reinvented. Voices closed in on me. I crossed and uncrossed my legs and then sneaked out of the crowd to land on a barstool back near the kitchen. A conversation fragment broke through.

"… and Mama's mother was white," my brother said.

I had a white grandmother?

The floor dropped away. I felt woozy. My mind reeled.

Am I … sort of … white? No. Can't be. I'm African American. An unacceptable shade of African. But … better to be insulted by your tribe than have no tribe at all.

When Mama's white mother was race-mixing with a colored man in the 1920s, her tribe likely fired insults at her.

White Grandmother, did my grandfather's people take you in? When their kin gathered, did you sneak to the back of the room?

Grandmother.

I don't remember you, but you lived long enough to caress my toddler cheek. The neutral expression I brought into this room … maybe, I mirrored it from you.

Did you sing me lullabies? Did you tell me secrets? Did you hold my hands while I learned to walk?

I followed my brother into the kitchen. "Mama's mother was white?"

"No," he said. "Mama's *grand*mother was white." She came over from—"

Oh.

A *great*-grandmother.

Great-grandmothers lived only as characters in family legends. They were creatures of our mythology, ghosts who drifted through our collective imagination.

White Grandmother, don't drift away. Tell me your secrets. Teach me how to walk.

My siblings and I flew in for my uncle's birthday. With us out-of towners around, the local cousins stopped by to catch up. By the time the last arrivals squeezed in, a trip to the restroom required advanced planning to map out a route over laps, knees, and feet.

I needed an air traffic controller to follow the chatter flying around.

"Hey, nobody noticed I'm not wearing …."

"… pregnant again … "

"… got a job with …"

"… and Mama's mother was white."

Hold up. Sounded like my brother, the family history expert, just said our mother's mother was white. Did everybody else already know?

I gauged the reaction in the room.

"... haven't needed 'em since cataract surgery … "

"… can't feed the kids they have … "

"… one of the airlines … "

I would have to work through my identity crisis on my own. The problem required top-level ethnicity math.

One white grandmother made me 25% white. And there had to be slavery-based dilution in the history of my other three grandparents … say 10% for each lineage … so add in another 30% for forced white inputs. There was also a white great-grandmother on my father's side. Another 12.5%. A double-great-grandfather in the maternal background on my paternal side—another 12.5%. This reduced my Negritude by 50%. I couldn't leave out my Blackfoot double-great-grandfather, so I subtracted 12.5% for Indigenous blood. My brother the expert could not identify our ancestors prior to the triple-great limb of the family tree. Therefore, in the interest of strict mathematical accuracy, I subtracted 23.3% for pre-substantiated non-blackness. That brought my total ethnicity down to minus eight percent. According to my calculations, I did not exist.

I crooked a finger at big brother and pointed him to the kitchen for a confab. "Did you say Mama's mother was white?"

"No," he said. "Mama's *grand*mother was white. Irish. Funny thing, most of our—"

Oh.

I followed him back to the living room, 1,000% sure my face was red.

DRIVE-BY CHILDHOOD

I pulled up at a red light, behind a delivery van. As a public radio pledge drive droned from an SUV idling in the left turn lane, deep male voices wafted through my open window. Three young black men were hanging out on the sidewalk, about to cross the street in the middle of traffic. On my left, a blast of hip-hop drowned out the pledge drive—a car cruising in the opposite direction had stopped for no reason I could discern. The young men shouted. They stepped off the curb. Toward my passenger side.

I slid my hand toward the buttons on the door but fought off the impulse to click the locks and close the windows.

The teenagers strolled right past my paranoid Honda, their laughter high-pitched and goofy, as they leaned into the window of the hip-hop car to bear hug their buddy.

Thank you, God. I'd resisted the urge to lock my doors, but there was no question I'd felt the urge.

I used to be a teenager. When I jaywalked, traffic always stopped for me. If my friends and I gossiped in the middle of the street, annoyed adult drivers steered around us. They probably went home and yelled at their own kids. Monday through Friday, I hid in my room in a cloud of incense, revived on Saturday night when the Jackson Five sang their ABCs and the party spilled into the driveway. Were the grown-ups next door trying to get some sleep?

The light turned green. Traffic sped into the intersection, peeled off right, left, and straight-ahead. I worried about those teenagers. Nowadays, annoyed adults might do more than drive past. An irritated driver might wave a gun to teach those children some manners. Had those babies' parents given them the talk? If you get stopped by the cops, hands in full view. Yes sir. No, sir.

I sent a meditation to the boys' reflection in my rear view mirror. "May you be happy. May you be peaceful. May you always make it to the other side of the street."

The Makeover

M y niece, Angelique, posted a photo of a ghoulish figurine on Facebook. In the description, she wrote *I'll have to get used to this new one. She looks a hot mess.*

"What the hell?" I asked my computer, when the photo came up in my feed.

The *she* was a bust: head, shoulders, and chest of a demon. Bulging white eyeballs with yellow pupils stared out from a face the color of pitch. The mouth gaped, swollen red lips pulled back from the gums, teeth bared like fangs. The monster's only arm bent at an unnatural angle in front of its mouth, like Frankenstein gripping a spoon. I couldn't tell whether the other arm was broken off or this was a one-armed fiend.

I had to look away, afraid this devil would terrorize me in a nightmare.

YouTube videos provided distraction. *Fifteen Fashion Hacks to Make You More Attractive. Five Ways You're Ruining Your Outfit. 5 Style Tips That No One Tells You!* Midway into "always cuff your sleeves," the demon's face began to seep back into my consciousness, and by the time the stylist demonstrated how to half-tuck your shirt, the video was obscured by the image of swollen red lips stretched back from teeth bared like fangs.

I clicked back to Angelique's post and rested my fingertips on the keyboard.

Wait a minute … it's not some devil … it's a person.

I leaned closer.

God. It's a woman.

A racist depiction of a black woman.

Of me.

I wanted to throw up.

I felt exposed. I was the monster. Mirrors distorted my reflection and tricked me into thinking I was a woman, while the world saw the real me, an ogre with a twisted limb poised in a macabre pantomime. I felt powerless to reclaim my flesh-and-blood womanhood.

Powerlessness brings with it an insistence on immediate action, in order to deflect attention from feelings. Research, Dawn. Put that master's degree to work. Use your intelligence to rebuild your power. Find out who created this atrocity and why.

Refseek dot com, an academic research browser, led me to an auction website specializing in racist collectibles—a combination of words that collided with my naïveté. Did the buyers collect racism in their homes and dust it off when they wanted to enjoy it?

Thinking maybe Angelique's find was a version of Mammy, I scrolled through that section, row after row of Mammies: ash trays, salt shakers, cookie jars, fishing lures, candles, rag dolls, cutting boards. They blurred one into the next. I sped past the Mammies, paused at the beginning of the lawn jockey section, before whipping through the postcard section, then movie posters. By the time I got to the last page of the auction site, I longed wistfully for Mammy. In her dependable white apron, she began to feel less like an assault and more like an annoyance—some distant relative you're embarrassed to be related to, because she always shows up in a head rag. I succumbed to comparative debasement. Mammy wasn't as bad as a pancake-pushing Aunt Jemima, which wasn't as bad as a watermelon-slurping pickaninny, which wasn't as bad as a photo of four naked black toddlers sitting on a riverbank—captioned "Alligator Bait."

Dazed, I forgot what I was looking for in the first place.

A click back to Facebook reminded me. The monster still held a place at the top of Angelique's page. I winced and grabbed the edge of the screen, ready to slam the laptop shut.

White girls at my grade school tied their straight hair in matching ponytails with pretty bows. They smiled pretty smiles, but not at me. I was the colored girl. I had a crush on a boy who sat in front of me. He twisted around with a note in his hand. When I reached for it, he turned into a horror movie victim—recoiled from my bulging lips, yellow eyes, bared fangs—and passed the note to a blonde classmate behind me.

On the auction website, I finally found the bust—a mechanical "Jolly Nigger Bank," designed for children. A back view showed a lever. Push the lever; the arm moved up to the open mouth, dropping a coin through the lips, as the eyes rolled back in the head. Close-up inspection showed it was one-armed on purpose, not broken. Circa 1890. Cast iron, made to last. The bottom read, "Manufactured by The J&E Stevens Co. Cromwell Conn. USA."

A piggy bank, purchased by an ordinary daddy, who set the gift on his kitchen table and showed his precious sugarplum how to push the lever. When Jolly Nigger swallowed her penny, sugarplum clapped.

What I wouldn't give to smash that cast iron bigotry over—.

Here I go again, playing out a revenge fantasy. I'd been mad so often. With such intensity. With no result. No peace. The piggy bank drained the fight out of me.

In the end, revenge felt as sickening as shame. What I really craved was for the daddy to reach across generations and say, "I'm sorry."

Won't someone in charge please say, "I'm sorry."

Absent an apology, I ended up infected with the hatred J&E Stevens fired into its cast iron toy. A father plunked down coins to buy the trinket for his daughter, and I reeled from his contempt a hundred years later. I loathed the daughter who delighted in the gift, as deeply as my classmate despised me the moment he passed his note to the blonde girl. I hated the endless supply of Mammies and Aunt Jemimas and lawn jockeys and Jolly Niggers on the auction website. I hated myself for being born the object of hatred, and then I hated having to reason, research, and revenge my way back to feeling human.

I was a hot mess.

My computer chimed a message from Angelique.

She'd posted another photo. "I've given Miss Hot Mess a makeover. Presenting Jazzy." Angelique had wrapped pink beads around the Frankenstein arm and plopped a pink bow atop the head.

I fought back a lump in my throat.

Where I had seen a monster, she'd seen Jazzy.

Where I'd seen racism, she'd seen Jazzy.

Where I'd seen contempt, she'd seen Jazzy.

These parallel realities called for a re-read of Angelique's initial post. She said she'd spied the castoff on the sidewalk, on a trip to the corner market. She'd picked it up and taken it home to join Mammy figurines she'd rescued over the years. (Decades earlier, I'd also collected Mammies, to get them off the market. After my interest had waned, I'd gotten rid of them, slipping them right back onto the market. Now this, an unwelcome affection for Mammy, bridging generations to create a bond between my niece and me.) Angelique's post read, *I'll have to get used to this new one. She looks a hot mess.*

There's a world of difference between looking a hot mess and being one.

Day after week after month after year of my walk through life, the sun rose on cynicism and set on hopelessness. Angelique's act of redemption blew me out of orbit. I collided with Jazzy—her beauty revealed, her humanity restored.

Impervious to the history that demoralized me, Jazzy didn't crave a different past.

The computer grew hot in my lap.

Heat. n. The transfer of energy from one body to another. (*Freedictionary dot com.*)

I closed the screen.

After digging through baubles stuffed in a dresser drawer, I wrapped my wrist in beads and tied a bow around my locks.

EPILOGUE

SAY THEIR NAMES

While I was writing a book about being black, other black people were killed.

Trevor Williams. Darrion Barnhill. Nana Adomako. Chad Robertson. Raynard Burton. Alteria Woods. Jordan Edwards. Tashii Brown. Aaron Bailey. Dejuan Guillory. Brian Easley. Isaiah Tucker. Patrick Harmon. Charles David Robinson. Devin Howell. Anthony Antonio Ford. Dewboy Lister. Calvin Toney. Lawrence Hawkins. Keita O'Neil. Jean Pedro Pierre. Arthur McAfee Jr. Ronell Foster. Shermichael Ezeff. Cameron Hall. Stephon Clark. Danny Thomas. Juan Markee Jones. Marcus-David L. Peters. Maurice Granton. Antwon Rose. Anthony Marcell Green. Robert Lawrence White. Rashaun Washington. Botham Jean. DeAndre Ballard. Emantic "EJ" Fitzgerald Bradford Jr. Jemel Roberson. Andre Horton. Jonathan Hart. Darius Tarver. Jimmy Atchison. D'Ettrick Griffin. Willie McCoy. Pamela Turner. Miles Hall. Ryan Twyman. JaQuavion Slaton. Brandon Webber. Eric Logan. De'Von Bailey. Elijah McClain. Christopher Whitfield. Atatiana Jefferson. Ariane McCree. Michael Dean. Jamee Johnson. Kwame "KK" Jones. Samuel David Mallard. William Green. Ahmaud Arbery. Breonna Taylor. Steven Demarco Dreasjon Reed. Finan H. Berhe. Yassin Mohamed. George Floyd. Natosha "Tony" McDade. David McAtee. Rayshard Brooks.

ABOUT THE AUTHOR

Dawn Downey is the author of three previous essay collections: *Searching for My Heart, From Dawn to Daylight,* and *Stumbling toward the Buddha.*

Her work has also been published in *Noteworthy: the Journal Blog; Persimmon Tree; punctuate.; River, Blood, and Corn Literary Journal; The Resilient Activist;* and *ZORA.*

A Downey day begins with meditation, followed by yoga—which moved from studio to dining room, after yoga teachers moved online in the year of self-quarantine. For additional well-being and to protect her writing time, she deploys an app that blocks political websites from her computer. She cheats by checking her tablet.

She misses in-person book events, the sharing of breath, and common experience.

Kansas City, Missouri is her home.

Learn more at DawnDowneyBlog.com.